Little Pebble™

Our Amazing Senses

Our Eyes Can See

by Jodi Wheeler-Toppen

CAPSTONE PRESS
a capstone imprint

Little Pebble is published by Capstone Press,
1710 Roe Crest Drive, North Mankato, Minnesota 56003
www.mycapstone.com

Library of Congress Cataloging-in-Publication Data
Names: Wheeler-Toppen, Jodi, author.
Title: Our eyes can see / by Jodi Wheeler-Toppen.
Description: North Mankato, Minnesota : Capstone Press, [2018] | Series: Our
    amazing senses | Audience: Age 4-7. | Audience: K to grade 3. | Includes
    bibliographical references and index.
Identifiers: LCCN 2017005234
ISBN 9781515767145 (library binding)
ISBN 9781515767190 (paperback)
ISBN 9781515767244 (eBook PDF)
Subjects: LCSH: Eye—Juvenile literature. | Vision—Juvenile literature. |
    Senses and sensation—Juvenile literature.
Classification: LCC QP475.7 .W46 2018 | DDC 612.8/4—dc23
LC record available at https://lccn.loc.gov/2017005234

Editorial Credits
Abby Colich, editor; Juliette Peters, designer; Wanda Winch, media researcher;
Tori Abraham, production specialist

Photo Credits
iStockphoto: rdegrie, 17; Shutterstock: agsandrew, motion design element, Designua, 9,
Dragon Images, cover, ESB Professional, 19, Grigorita Ko, 21, Hatchapong Palurtchaivong,
11, iconogenic, 13, Peter Hermes Furian, 7, Peter Kotoff, 1, photoJS, 15, Pichugin Dmitry, 5

Printed in the United States   5669

Table of Contents

Look and See

Look! A tree!

See the shape.

See the colors.

How You See

Light hits the tree.

The light bounces.

It hits a lens in your eye.

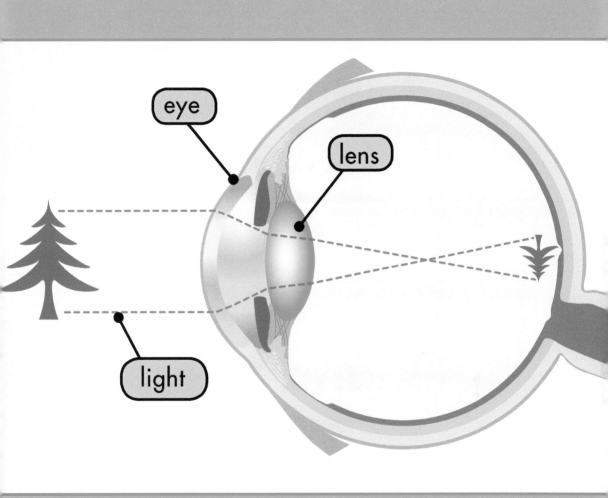

eye

lens

light

The lens bends the light.

The light hits your retina.

The retina has rods.

It has cones.

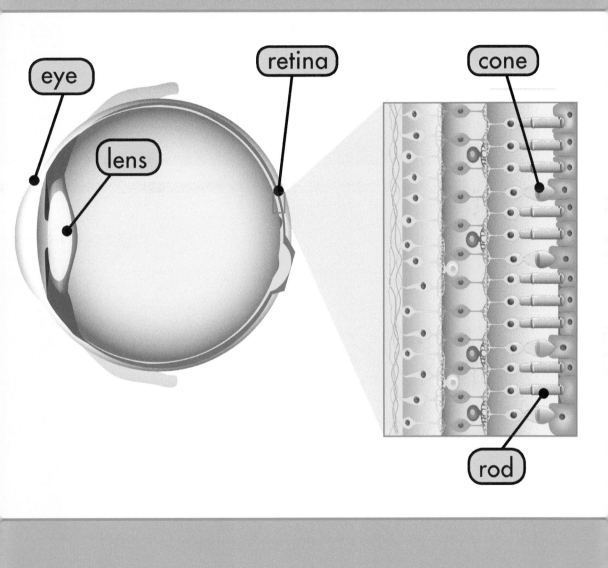

eye

lens

retina

cone

rod

Rods see shape.

Cones see color.

They signal your brain.

It's a tree you see!

Eye Parts

Look in a mirror.

See the color?

That's your iris.

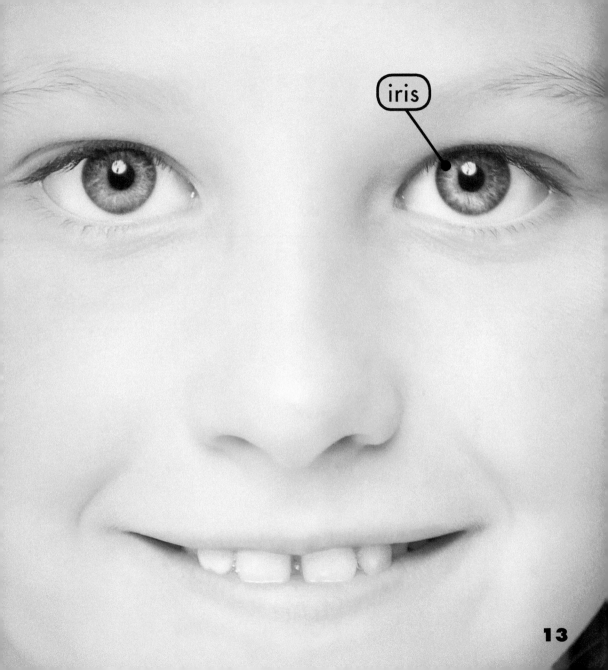

iris

See the dark circle?

It is your pupil.

It lets light into your eye.

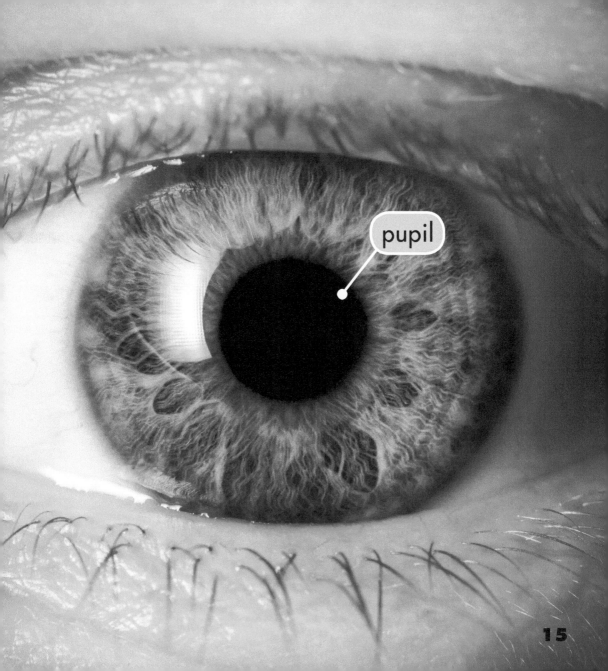

pupil

Go into a dark room.

Your eyes need
more light to see.

Your pupils get big.

They let in more light.

Go outdoors.

Wow! The sun is bright.

Your pupils get small.

They let in just a little light.

Your eyes let you see
all around you.
Look! A cat. **Meow!**
It is white. See it run.

Glossary

brain—the organ inside your head that controls your movements, thoughts, and feelings

cone—tiny part in eye that lets you see colors

iris—the round, colored part of your eye

lens—the clear part of the eye that covers the pupil

pupil—the round, dark center of your eye that lets in light

retina—the lining inside the back of the eyeball

rod—a tiny part in the eye that lets you see shapes

signal—a message between the brain and the senses

Read More

Appleby, Alex. *What I See.* My Five Senses. New York: Gareth Stevens Publishing, 2015.

Dayton, Connor. *Sight.* Your Five Senses and Your Sixth Sense. New York: PowerKids Press, 2014.

Murray, Julie. *I Can See.* Senses. Minneapolis, Minn.: Abdo Kids, 2016.

Internet Sites

Use FactHound to find Internet sites related to this book.

Visit *www.facthound.com*
Type in this code: 9781515767145

Check out projects, games and lots more at
www.capstonekids.com

Critical Thinking Questions

1. Reread page 8. Use the glossary to define *retina*.

2. What do cones see? What do rods see?

3. What would happen if you had no pupils?

Index